THE NUCLEAR WINTER MAN

WESTERN ISLES
LIBRARIES

30299858J

J001.9

BY

TERRY DEARY

Kingfis

D1580667

KINGFISHER
An imprint of Larousse plc
Elsley House
24–30 Great Titchfield Street
London W1P 7AD

Copyright © Larousse plc 1996
Text copyright © Terry Deary 1996

First published by Larousse plc 1996

10 9 8 7 6 5 4 3 2 1

A CIP catalogue record this book is available from the British Library

ISBN 0 7534 0065 0

Terry Deary has asserted his moral right to be identified as the author of
the work in accordance with the Copyright, Designs and Patents Act, 1988.

"You will have to make your own minds up about how much of the facts
contained in this story are true. Some are based on public information, but
others are the result of a fictional interpretation by the author of events, what
might have been said or done. Some names have been changed, as you can
see, to protect the individuals involved."

Printed in the United Kingdom

CONTENTS PAGE

INTRODUCTION

Thousands of people disappear each year. Some commit suicide in remote places, and their bodies are never found. Some, dissatisfied with their lives, choose to vanish without trace from their homes, changing their names and inventing new lives for themselves elsewhere. But occasionally more sinister disappearances occur. Solitary travellers or homeless people are murdered by thieves, gangsters or kidnappers, and their bodies well-concealed.

However, a rarer kind of missing person is the one who is 'removed' by a government which finds his or her views disagreeable. Such a person might be paid a large sum of money in return for leaving the country and taking on a new identity. More likely, however, he or she becomes the victim of forces – agents and professional assassins – operating in the shadowy world of espionage.

Last of all is the defector – the person who leaves his or her country for another, changing identity in the process. Doctor Vladimir Alexandrov, a Russian scientist convinced that a nuclear war would lead to disastrous climactic change, may well have fallen into this category. He disappeared while at a conference in Spain in 1985, and to this day his fate remains a mystery. Did he strike up a deal with the CIA to defect to America? Or was he 'liquidated' by the KGB, who found his views inconvenient? One KGB officer was determined to find the answers to these questions. Possibly they lay in a secret file, a file marked:

CLASSIFIED

CHAPTER ONE

"We've lost a scientist," the Colonel said.

I wanted to say, 'That's careless,' but I'd heard all about the Colonel. His idea of humour was pulling the legs off flies. He was short and bald-headed, and so fat he seemed about to burst from his ill-fitting uniform.

"Yes, comrade," I said instead.

"His name's Vladimir Alexandrov. He's an expert on climate."

"Oh," I said. It was hard to get worked up over a cloud-watcher.

"Alexandrov is one of the world's greatest experts on 'Nuclear Winter'," the Colonel went on. He rose from behind his desk and waddled round to lean against the table in front of me. I looked down at the carpet, which was red-brown with the *gul* flower pattern of Turkestan. To have a carpet like that distinguished the owner as one of the KGB élite.

"You've heard of Nuclear Winter, I suppose?" he said.

"Certainly. About two years ago some scientists in America came up with a theory that a war fought with nuclear weapons would be a disaster. It would plunge the world into some sort of permanent winter that would destroy all life on Earth. They tried to persuade their government to cut their stocks of nuclear weapons..."

I saw that the Colonel's trousers, which were too short for him, had hitched up to reveal socks of a particularly virulent shade of purple.

"Do you know where those nuclear weapons would be targeted?" he said.

"On our cities, comrade?"

"Naturally! But in particular on *Moscow*," he said. Then he pointed up to the ceiling. "Nuclear warheads would explode in the air only a few kilometres above this office. The radiation would travel at the speed of light and set fire to buildings up to 15 kilometres from the city centre. But the fires wouldn't burn for long. You know why?"

"No, comrade." Studying the disastrous effects of nuclear war wasn't exactly my idea of bedtime reading.

"The shock wave from the blast would blow out the fires."

He paused as if waiting for me to say something.

"Is that good?" I said at last.

"Oh, *very* good," he snorted. "The same shock wave would flatten every building in the city. The Kremlin here would be dust. The Granovitaya Palace is five hundred years old. All that history would be completely wiped out in seconds."

"I see," I said, thinking that a few million human beings, though obviously not as valuable as the Granovitaya Palace, would be wiped out too.

"Then, of course," went on my instructor, "there would be the mushroom cloud, formed by the dust drawn up into the lower stratosphere. More fires would start up from broken gas pipes and so on, and oxygen would be sucked in at a huge rate. Hurricane winds would rush in to fan the flames and you'd have an enormous inferno."

"Like Hiroshima?"

"Much, much worse. This would be the greatest fire the world had ever seen. And when everything flammable had gone up there'd be a soot cloud hovering over thousands of square kilometres. It would blot out the Sun and turn day into night. No Sun means no warmth. Permanent winter. Nuclear winter."

2

"But America would be in the same state," I countered. "If they attacked us, then our missiles would rain down on them. We might even win the war."

The Colonel leaned forward and stared at me with bulging, bloodshot eyes. I could smell vodka on his breath.

"Our missing scientist, the good Doctor Alexandrov, argues that *everyone* in the world would lose in such a war. Without light, the vegetation would die. Without plants, the animals would die, and without plants or animals, the human race..."

"I think I get the idea," I said.

He leaned back and spread his pudgy hands on his thighs.

"Well, you needn't worry about Nuclear Winter, Velikhov," he said, smiling slyly.

"Why not?" I said, knowing the answer.

"You'll be dead. Within ten seconds of the first missile exploding over Moscow. The long-term effects of a nuclear war therefore would be of no concern to you."

He seemed to enjoy that little joke. He, of course, along with the rest of top brass, would be safe in a blast-proof shelter underneath the Kremlin.

He turned to his desk and picked up a thin folder.

"Take this back to your office and study it. It'll give you a start in your search for Alexandrov."

He passed the folder across. There could hardly have been a dozen sheets inside; it was no doubt only a fraction of the the Alexandrov file. But that's how the KGB works: only give your agents as much as they need to know.

"Why me, comrade?"

The Colonel frowned; agents didn't usually ask 'why'.

"You're young, and you've never had an assignment outside Moscow. We think it's time you spread your wings.

We are giving you responsibility. Do well, and you can earn a promotion."

"And if I fail?"

"Fail?" he repeated incredulously. "Velikhov, it would seem that an ability to ask questions, even stupid ones, is your strong point. I suspect you will have to ask a lot of them if you are going to track down Alexandrov. However, in the impossible event of your failure, it will not matter too much. The Doctor carries no state or military secrets. We want to know what's become of him, that's all."

I didn't believe that for a moment. The KGB considered everything it did, no matter how trivial, absolutely vital to Soviet security.

"Remember we have a new President," the Colonel continued, with an air of living in wondrous times. "Comrade Gorbachev is our youngest leader for over 50 years. He has spoken to us. He wants us to give youth a chance. You are young and..."

"I understand the comrade President is also talking about *glasnost* – openness," I broke in. "In which case I would only mention that there are, perhaps, some papers missing from this folder. I thought, comrade – in the interests of openness of course – you might permit me to see them."

The Colonel rose from his chair with a sigh. He waddled to the door and held it open for me.

"There are some things, Velikhov," he said as I drew level with him, "which must remain secret even to someone of your earth-shaking talents."

Then, unexpectedly, his expression became almost wistful.

"Young man, you have a future in the KGB. One day – who knows? Perhaps nothing that goes on in our country

4

will be a secret to you. Maybe then..." and he looked down at his shoes, "you will wish it was."

CHAPTER TWO

The file on Doctor Alexandrov was notable as much for what it did *not* say as for what it did. It told me he was born into a peasant family on New Years' Day, 1938, in the Ukraine, and that he graduated from Moscow Physical Technical Institute in 1961; that in the 1960s he worked on experimental physics for the military; and that in 1985 he disappeared while staying in Madrid, Spain.

One other date caught my eye. Early in 1983 a group of American scientists put a request through their embassy in Moscow. They were planning a 'closed' conference, scientists only, to discuss the effects of nuclear war, and it obviously wouldn't be complete without some contribution from the USSR. The request was made ten weeks in advance.

I stopped pacing my uncarpeted office floor and laughed. Give ten *months* warning and you might just get a Soviet scientist. I knew KGB procedures. Before one of our experts could travel to the West we'd have to check him out thoroughly. It was the sort of job I'd done before. I had to assess how much the applicant knew – and whether he'd defect. How many Soviet secrets could he take with him? What was his political record? Was he a loyal Party man or a trouble-maker? How would he react to a spell in the West?

There were of course ways to make sure of someone's return. For example, we could use a loving wife and children as insurance ('hostages' seems such an ugly word). We'd let the expert know that if he didn't come back, his family would get an extended holiday in Siberia.

6

On the other hand, an unhappily married man did not get a visa. He had too many reasons *not* to come home.

All this research into a man's background took time. Ten months to a year was normal. But *ten weeks*! That was the first surprise of the Alexandrov case. The Soviet Academy of Sciences recommended he should go to this Nuclear Winter conference in Massachusetts, USA, and he'd received almost immediate clearance.

Then I had my second shock. It seemed the Doctor had been a frequent visitor to the USA. He spoke good English and had worked both at the National Center for Atmospheric Research in Colorado and at Oregon State University. He'd adapted US programmes for our computers in Moscow.

The authorization for these visits had apparently been given by the Director of the KGB himself. However, there was no explanation for this untypically liberal attitude.

Fine. So perhaps the KGB had simply decided he was 'low risk' and unlikely to fall victim to all the temptations of the West. Nevertheless, 'low risk' or not, such a person would at least have had a junior KGB 'minder' assigned to accompany them.

So I decided my first enquiries should be with this 'minder', whoever he was. The chances were he could be found in the Kremlin here – unless he were abroad on another case.

Then I had my third surprise. Checking the back of the file, where such things are usually recorded, I found a blank space against the word 'Escort'. Alexandrov had *no* minder!

That just didn't happen. Did this man really exist, and if he did, was he actually *Russian*?

A recent photograph also worried me. Alexandrov was a

7

Party member, yet he dressed like a capitalist businessman; the suit he wore looked as though it would cost me a year's wages. Where did a Soviet scientist get that kind of money? And why was he allowed to flaunt it so openly?

On another page was a form, typewritten, with a request from Alexandrov himself. It seemed that the Nuclear Winter conference had been a success. The Americans had persuaded their politicians of the terrible consequences of a nuclear war. They urged Alexandrov to try out their calculations on his computer back in Moscow. The form was an application for time on the Soviet computers to run his tests.

Computer time is strictly limited; also, the computers contain secrets that need to be protected. Vladimir Alexandrov wanted access at short notice – it seemed there was to be another conference in Washington just six months after the first one. In theory there was no chance of him getting approval: there was a waiting list of over a year. To get in first he would have to push someone else out of the queue.

No sooner had I thought that than I read the scrawled signature of the Director at the bottom of Vladimir Alexandrov's application and the word: 'Approved'.

Who *was* this man? I picked up the phone and dialled the next office. "Andrei?" I asked.

"You woke me up, Yuri," he complained. I grinned; Andrei liked to put on a show of lazy disregard, but his mind was razor-sharp. He was the only person on our floor as young as me but he'd been in the KGB for two years longer. I often went to him for advice. "Tell me about 1983," I began.

"After '82 and before '84," he yawned.

"Ha ha. Tell me about our interest in nuclear war at that

8

time."

He drew in a deep breath. "Reagan was President of the United States," he droned. "Defence Secretary was Casper Weinberger. He came up with the amazing statement that a limited nuclear war was 'winnable'. That made us think the US might be planning one. Things were very tense at the time. In September we shot down one of their airliners when it strayed into Soviet air space."

"I remember," I said. "But what were we doing about this nuclear business?"

"We set up Operation Ryan. We started to look for signs that the West was building up to a nuclear war – one where they could strike first and win."

"What signs, exactly?"

"Oh, unusual stockpiles of blood plasma in emergency units, military establishments working longer hours than normal, that sort of thing."

"And what did we discover?" I persisted.

"The US was being its usual aggressive self, but not planning anything specific. Now, with Gorbachev running things, the atmosphere in this regard has cooled off a good deal."

"Thanks, Andrei. You're a gold mine."

"Sure, sure. Now, do you mind? I've got some sleep to catch up on."

The file, short on facts as it was, raised more questions than it gave answers. I decided it was time I talked to some people who knew this shadow man, Alexandrov. I'd start with his family. Making a note of the address – Arkhipov Street, a short walk across the city – I headed for the door.

Chapter Three

From the outside, the Alexandrovs' apartment block looked as grim and prison-like as most buildings of its kind in Moscow. The windows were no more than slits in the wintry grey concrete and the entrance resembled a tunnel. A small pale woman opened the door to No. 6.

"Mrs Alexandrov?" I said. She looked me over, I thought, a little scornfully.

"KGB?" she said.

"KGB."

She didn't invite me in, she just turned her back to me and left the door open.

I had expected the usual shoebox of a flat, with bare floors and cheap furniture. Quite the reverse – the interior was richly upholstered with oriental rugs and cushions, there were bookcases stuffed with foreign editions and real oil paintings on the walls. Western rock music resounded in one of the rooms. The woman saw me looking towards it and explained. "My daughter, Olga. She likes..."

I smiled. "The Rolling Stones, by the sound of it."

She set her lips. I could see she thought this was the prelude to some kind of trick. A KGB agent, it seemed, wasn't human enough to enjoy any kind of music, let alone decadent western 'pop'.

"Olga! Turn your music off and come in here!" called the woman.

"You have some fine foreign books," I said.

"It's my job," she said defensively. "I do some reviewing and translating."

The music stopped suddenly and her daughter appeared.

10

The file said she was 16. Like her mother, Olga had dark hair and wide-set, anxious-looking eyes. She coughed as she sat on the edge of a chair.

"Olga has asthma," her mother explained, "while I, simply, am old. But you of course have come about Vladimir."

"Have you heard from him?"

She shook her head. "We thought *you* might know. Perhaps you had taken Vladimir in for questioning."

"And why would we do that, Mrs Alexandrov?" I asked.

She looked at me as if that scarcely merited an answer.

"The way he disappeared," she said at last. She was insinuating something that *I* was not prepared to answer.

"He could have defected to the United States," I said instead.

"No!" she cried. "I am not well. And Olga... He would never leave us. Never!"

I'd questioned many suspects in my year or so with the KGB, and I prided myself that I could always spot a liar. The Alexandrov woman wasn't lying.

"In that case, perhaps you could help me find him."

"They've stopped paying us!" the girl put in.

"What was that?"

"They've stopped father's pay. They always do that when they think someone's defected. We are having to live on our savings."

"Vladimir would know that," her mother added. "He'd never leave us in that position."

"Tell me everything you know about his disappearance," I said. "What have you got to lose? We both want to find him, don't we?"

There was a moment's silence.

"And if the CIA have kidnapped him?" Olga said.

"Is that what you think happened?"

11

"Yes."

"And why would *they* do that?"

"Because he knew too much."

"About what?"

"Nuclear Winter," she said.

"Tell me."

The girl wandered over and sat next to her mother on the sofa.

"The American computers are more advanced than ours..." Mrs Alexandrov began, looking at me to see if she had committed an indiscretion.

"Go on."

"Well, Vladimir needed a powerful computer to calculate the effects of changes on the atmosphere. The Americans let him use their Cray computer. He once said the Cray could run one of his programmes in six minutes – our computers take 48 *hours*. He went to America eight times, you know. He's been going there since 1978."

"Did he get a taste for American life?"

Mrs Alexandrov could see where a question like that might lead, but decided to be straight.

"Vladimir admired it even before he went there. American films, novels, food – even hamburgers."

"But he loved Russia too," Olga broke in. "All his friends were here."

"Yes," her mother said, her face softening at the memory. "This flat has seen many wonderful parties."

"What work did he do in the 1970s?" I asked suddenly. The question seemed to surprise her.

"He worked for the Computing Centre in the Soviet Academy of Science. His boss was Nikita Moiseev himself."

Moiseev was a powerful man, with friends, as they say, in the highest circles. He was the sort of man who could easily arrange to get Doctor Alexandrov free passage to and from the USA.

"And when the American nuclear scientists invited him to the conference..."

"They didn't," Mrs Alexandrov said. "Well, not exactly. You see, in a way, he invited himself."

The Alexandrov case, which I had taken on with little enthusiasm, was becoming stranger by the minute.

"Go on," I said again.

Chapter Four

It seemed that in 1977 Doctor Alexandrov had gone to a conference on climate in Tashkent in the south of the Soviet Union. There he met some eminent US professors from Oregon University, and persuaded them that he was important enough to invite to the States.

I interrupted Mrs Alexandrov. "Your husband, apparently, spoke good English."

"Yes. Very good."

"Even though he'd never been to an English-speaking country?"

"He wanted to speak to foreign scientists," the scientist's wife explained.

Or he wanted to be ready to defect, I thought. "So he went to Oregon in 1977?" I prompted.

"Yes. He kept in touch through our San Francisco consulate."

The consulate was, I knew, a centre for gathering information on the US.

"Was he away for long during each trip?" I asked.

"Sometimes a few months," she shrugged.

"You must have been lonely," I suggested, hoping to hear more about their relationship. Her answer surprised me.

"Yes. But once I was able to join him when he went out there in 1980."

Another fact missing from the file. A Russian scientist would not take his wife on foreign trips – not unless he was specially privileged or a spy playing happy families. Mrs Alexandrov would have made a perfect 'cover' for an agent.

"Did you enjoy the trip?" I asked.

"I missed my home," she replied with emphasis. She exchanged a pained look with her daughter.

"What is it?" I asked.

The woman twisted her thin, pale hand in her lap before continuing. "The KGB probably read my mail anyway… to see if I am in touch with Vladimir… So, I may as well show you the letter I am writing to Senator Kennedy in the United States. You can tell me if I'll be allowed to send it."

Olga rose and walked to her mother's writing desk and took a sheet of paper from the top drawer.

The letter was in English and my own English was good enough to let me understand it. It read:

Dear Sir,

The wife of Soviet scientist Vladimir Alexandrov appeals to you. My husband, as you may know, disappeared on March 31, 1985 in Madrid, Spain. I ask you, in the name of common humanity, to ask your government what information, if any, they have relating to him. His disappearance is inexplicable: Vladimir Alexandrov loves his country and his family, and I cannot imagine he would stay away from them by choice. Let me say, I have the fullest confidence in your good faith in this matter. Yours, etc.

"It can do no harm to send it," I said.

Mrs Alexandrov took the letter from me. "Thank you."

"So you do believe that your husband's in America. Why?"

She did not answer. Up to now, I had been soft with her; it was time to apply a little pressure.

"You know, he could have been attacked by Spanish criminals. Robbed and left for dead," I suggested. Olga

15

clutched at her mother's arm, who straightened her back and said, "I am sure the Spanish police would have found some trace of him."

"I hope so," I said and rose to my feet.

"What will *you* do?" she asked.

"Go to Spain. The answer to this little mystery lies somewhere on the streets of Madrid."

Chapter Five

"You want to go to Spain!" the Colonel shouted. "It may surprise you to learn we have an embassy there. And in that embassy we have a perfectly good agent. He's come up with nothing. Why should we waste money sending *you*?"

"Our agent in Madrid," I said quietly, "has simply reported that the Spanish authorities are not co-operating. But no one can disappear without trace. It seems to me our agent in the embassy has failed to do a proper job. Someone, comrade, I would most respectfully suggest, should go down there and shake things up."

The Colonel turned his back on me and with clasped hands looked out of his window towards the Academy of Sciences at the end of Gorky Park.

"Well, as Comrade Gorbachev is always saying," he muttered with barely concealed sarcasm, "we must encourage youth."

He turned back to me. "Well, go to Madrid then. Look for our Doctor Alexandrov. And while you're there, compile a report on Lieutenant Grushkov, our agent in the embassy."

"I though you said he was 'perfectly good?' "

"Young man, if you want a future handing out parking tickets, continue to say things like that."

"Yes, comrade."

"And while you're in Madrid, will you please account for every rouble you spend."

The KGB had an obsession with accounting.

"Peseta, comrade. They use pesetas in Spain."

The Colonel thumped the table with his fist. "Velikhov,

we are a country at war. Or should I say, we could be..."

"Yes, comrade."

He sat down and looked at me searchingly.

"You've never killed a man, have you?" he said.

"No, I have not."

"And do think you would have trouble doing it, if ordered to?"

It was something I had often thought about. Obviously we had all been trained in the many ways to take a human life, but that in no way prepared you for the act itself. I decided to make my answer as neutral as I could.

"If it was for the good of the State..." I began.

"Velikhov," interrupted the Colonel, "it is *always* 'for the good of the State'. This Alexandrov business... If you should discover Comrade Grushkov has collaborated with western agents in any way, I want him removed, do you understand?"

I understood only too well. Not for the first time had I suspected the Colonel of holding something back. The elimination order for Grushkov seemed unnecessary – unless of course the Colonel already knew what part he'd played in Alexandrov's disappearance. However, I decided this was no time for questions.

"Yes, comrade," I said simply.

"Take a pistol from the armoury," he said, scribbling on a permit. "And a thousand roubles. Bring receipts back for everything. As for your flight – economy class."

"Thank you so much, comrade. But clothes? I may stand out a little in Madrid in this," I said, picking at the lapel of my iron-grey, KGB-issue suit.

Irritably, he pulled out more forms. I gathered my sheaf of papers and headed for the door.

"Velikhov!" the Colonel called. "I want you back in two

weeks. Your report on Comrade Grushkov must be verbal, and to me only. And if you have to – you know, kindly do it discreetly. I don't want to open my selection of Western papers and see them plastered with embarrassing headlines. Relations with the West are going through a particularly sensitive stage. And I want to know immediately if you find Alexandrov. It may be necessary to..."

"Remove him too?" I said.

The Colonel stared at me a moment with his bloodshot eyes, then looked down at his hands.

"Whether Alexandrov's vanishing act was his fault or not," he said carefully, "it was most inconvenient. Also, we have no way of knowing what he was up to in his absence. He may have passed on details of our nuclear capability to our enemies."

For once the Colonel's reasons seemed plausible. So why did I feel, as I left him in his office, that I was being used for some darker purpose?

Chapter Six

Stepping off the plane in Madrid was like walking into a furnace. The heat hit me solidly; my shirt was soaked with sweat before I had even reached the arrivals lounge.

A square man with a square, greasy, pock-marked face came forward at the gate. He grabbed my hand.

"Grushkov?" I asked.

"Call me Anatoli," he chuckled.

We collected my case and loaded it into an embassy car. As we sat in the back Grushkov slapped my leg. "First time out of the Soviet Union?" he asked.

"Yes."

"But you're not Russian?"

"No. I'm from Georgia," I said.

"Ah!" he cried. "Me too!" and breathlessly he began to recall some of the places in our homeland that he knew well.

As he stepped out of the car he threw an arm over my shoulder, crushing me against him as we walked into the embassy.

"We must arrange to write good reports about each other," he chuckled again.

I failed to cover my confusion. "Reports?"

He raised his bushy eyebrows. "But of course! That is the way of the KGB. The Colonel sent you here to look for Doctor Alexandrov, but without doubt he also told you to report on me: that much is routine. Naturally, he also contacted me last night and told *me* to compile a report on *you*!" He laughed uproariously. I began to take a liking to this grinning lump of a man.

"Have a shower and change," he said. "There's a light meal waiting in your room. We'll meet in an hour and I'll have everything you want ready by then."

An hour later, refreshed and dressed in a summer suit purchased on KGB funds, I went down to the lounge to see Grushkov.

He was on the phone when I entered.

"Ah, Yuri!" he cried as I opened the door, and put his hand over the receiver. "Have a look at that book on the table there. I'm just contacting a few witnesses to Alexandrov's last days." He went back to his call.

It was a slim book in Russian, very recently published, with the snappy title *Climactic and Biological Consequences of Nuclear War*. I turned immediately to the credits to see what contribution Vladimir Alexandrov had made. The answer, curiously, appeared to be none. Nowhere in a Russian book on Nuclear Winter was our greatest expert mentioned.

Grushkov put down the phone and came over to the sofa opposite me.

"Well?" he asked.

"Well... it looks as if someone has already decided what happened to Vladimir Alexandrov," I said. "He never existed. He's become a non-person."

Grushkov nodded so vigorously that his jowls wobbled. "The KGB would only order that if they suspect he has defected to the United States," he said.

"Is that what you reported?"

He held up a hand. "I reported the few facts I had. Nothing else. I am trained to gather information, not interpret it. I am not a detective. That's your job, my boy. Your file..."

"You've read a file on me?" I asked.

He shrugged. "Of course. Now, the KGB have decided

21

that Vladimir Alexandrov has defected – unless of course you can come up with another explanation."

"I see." I looked at the book in my hands. I suddenly felt annoyance at the web of intrigue surrounding me. At its centre, I thought, sat the Colonel, like a great malignant spider. I made a decision.

"Anatoli... If we are agreed that we can collaborate on our reports, then perhaps we can also forget the formalities. We can talk off the record?"

His eyes sparkled. "I hope so."

"Then you can tell me – off the record – what you *think* happened. As well as about the factual report you sent back to Moscow."

"I can," he said briskly. "I think Alexandrov's days were numbered. He had risen into the sky like a rocket. His fame was worldwide. He was no longer a scientist. He was a *personality*. Now some rockets reach the atmosphere, and stay in orbit for a long time – great men like Albert Einstein for example. But some rockets don't quite make orbit velocity. You know what happens then?"

"They fall back to Earth," I said.

"Exactly. And they fall fast. Our friend Alexandrov was on course for self-destruction by the time he reached Madrid."

"But he was such an expert," I argued. "He'd met Senator Edward Kennedy."

Grushkov rocked with laughter. "Kennedy! He'd done a little better than that. He had gone in front of the US Congress to give evidence – a quite unique honour for a Soviet scientist. Then he was summoned to the Vatican in Rome. Pope John Paul II wanted to hear all about Nuclear Winter. He wrote articles, gave interviews – the whole thing."

"So what went wrong?" I asked.

22

"He was working with Soviet computers," Grushkov explained. "As you must know, our computers are toys compared to American ones."

"But he had access to their computers," I pointed out.

"For a while, yes. But when he was recently granted a visa by the US Embassy in Moscow, it was stamped with the condition: 'Not permitted direct or indirect access to the super-computers in the United States.'"

"Why?" I asked.

"Perhaps they suspected he was working for the KGB. Even *I* suspect that! Or perhaps it was simply that they had too many secrets on those computers."

"He must have been disappointed," I said.

"He was in fact far from disappointed. And he did something rather foolish. He boasted that the visa stamp was meaningless. He claimed he could have access to the super-computers whenever he wanted. He had influence in the US and nothing, or no one, could stop him." Grushkov shook his head. "Fame made him vain and foolish. He began to believe that he could bring about world peace himself. He wanted to travel the world telling of the horrors of Nuclear Winter and force governments to disarm."

"A prophet of doom," I said.

"More than that. He was a Soviet prophet. He was showing everyone how much the USSR agonized over nuclear weapons. That was good propaganda for us – bad for the US."

"So the CIA kidnapped him?"

Grushkov sighed. "I couldn't say. Alexandrov did not get access to US computers after his foolish boasting – the CIA made sure of that. He had to do his calculations in Moscow to check the results of the US scientists. His results contradicted a lot of what the US was saying... He believed things were worse, much worse! It would appear that science was moving on, but Alexandrov was standing still, and digging in his heels. While he was travelling the world painting a picture of nuclear catastrophe, his old friends in the US were revising their opinions entirely. In just a year he seemed, right or not, a sad has-been."

"But still respected in the Soviet Union – after all, he was pushing our line on Nuclear Winter – and he was a leading scientist."

"To some extent. But he had problems back home, too."

"So could the KGB have got rid of him?" I said, bewildered.

Grushkov laughed again.

"Again, I couldn't say. But one thing I do know. Alexandrov had reasons *not* to return to Moscow."

"So now you're saying he arranged his own disappearance?"

"Patience, my friend, patience. Let me tell you about the Doctor's last few months. Then you can draw your own conclusions."

CHAPTER SEVEN

Anatoli Grushkov took a bottle of Vodka from a cabinet and raised it to me. I shook my head; I needed a clear brain to solve this case. The old man poured himself a glass and drained it. He refilled it and placed the tumbler on the table in front of him.

"Too much talking," he smiled, "gives a man a thirst. Vladimir Alexandrov talked *and* had a great thirst too," he added after a pause.

"You're saying he was a drunk?"

"Let's just say he liked a drink. Until he arrived in Madrid it had never been a particular problem. But you must remember Alya Alexandrov, his wife."

"What about her?" I asked.

"She's ill. It seems she has a liver disease – cirrhosis. You know what causes it?" he asked.

"Drink," I replied.

"Exactly. To the Alexandrovs heavy drinking was normal. Of course Vladimir tried desperately to help his wife. He smuggled powerful drugs from America to help her. He took tissue samples to England to have them analyzed. He tried to get permission for Alya to accompany him to the West for treatment – but this time he was refused permission."

"But surely he'd want to get back to Moscow to help her. Surely he wouldn't just disappear at the time when his wife needed him most? The reports say he was devoted to her. What were the problems in Moscow that would keep him away?"

"The fear of failure," Anatoli said. "A sad condition. Worse

25

than cirrhosis! Vladimir Alexandrov had a meteoric rise, remember. He needed just one last boost to get him into the holy of holies – the Academy of Sciences. He'd then have funding for his research – and his expensive lifestyle – and access to the best computers. The trouble is he had to pass a test and be awarded what the scientists call a *doctorate*. The test was a five hour examination by the best scientists in the Soviet Union. They would try to pull his Nuclear Winter work apart and make him defend it. They would question every detail of what he did and why he was doing it. Even if he performed well he could still lose the doctorate on a secret vote."

"He had powerful friends," I argued, remembering the freedom he was given to travel the world.

"And he must have had powerful *enemies* too, remember. He would be most worried about his scientific work though. Alexandrov had spent a year travelling the world talking to presidents and popes like some travelling Nuclear Winter salesman. He wasn't doing much new work. His research and scientific knowledge hadn't advanced for many years. He was on his way back to face the five hour test when he stopped off here. He must have been reluctant to face the grilling."

"He'd done all his scientific investigation back in 1983, though. He should have been given credit for that."

"*No* one was giving him credit for that any more, not even his old American friends. An article had been published in the US magazine called *Science*. It had been quite a cruel attack on Soviet Nuclear Winter research and, of course, that meant Vladimir Alexandrov's work in particular."

"What did it say?"

Anatoli ticked off the points on his stubby fingers. "One,

that Alexandrov's theory was based on US research; two, that the research itself was long out of date; three, that the claims the scientists make are exaggerated; four, that they are adding nothing new to the world's knowledge; and five, the Soviets were not putting much effort into Nuclear Winter research. The article title said it all... *Soviets offer little help.*"

I nodded. "Moscow wouldn't be very pleased with that. When he got home he'd probably never be allowed out again."

"Strangely, he was. He was allowed out that one last time to go to a meeting in Cordoba. He arrived here on Friday March 29... at least he arrived at Barajas airport where I picked you up. There had been visa problems so he was a day late. It was an extra strain. Instead of having a day's rest before giving his speech he was to be taken straight to Cordoba by the City Hall car."

"So he didn't come to the Embassy?"

Anatoli grinned. "He did, because I picked him up instead."

"Why?"

He shrugged. "Because I was told to. There was an instruction from Moscow for him to get in touch. He couldn't use an open telephone line from the airport. He had to be brought here to use a secure phone. So I went to the airport and kidnapped him."

"You *what*...!"

"Ha! Only joking, my friend. There was the driver from Cordoba waiting for him. I just tapped the driver on the shoulder and told him we needed to bring Vladimir Alexandrov back here first. The Cordoba driver is a man called José Moreno. When I heard you were coming to investigate I asked Moreno to come here for questioning.

27

He's in a waiting room now. Let me know when you want to speak to him."

"You're very efficient, comrade," I said.

He made a mock bow. "Perhaps that will go in your report on me. And perhaps you will not need to use that gun under your jacket after all."

CHAPTER EIGHT

José Moreno was nervous. Who could blame him? He'd been questioned by the Spanish police, but they hadn't been too interested in his story. When he heard the KGB wanted to talk to him, Moreno must have feared harsher treatment. He entered the room as if he was going to have a chat with the Spanish Inquisition.

He carried his uniform cap but was twisting it nervously. He was a small man with sharp, foxy features, and his dark eyes darted around the room. "Ah! José!" Anatoli cried cheerfully in Spanish; fortunately I had passing knowledge of the language. "My friend! Remember me?"

"You are the gentleman who met me at the airport and took my scientist passenger," he said, guardedly.

"José! I didn't *take* him from you. I simply had to bring him here to make a phone call."

The man stuck out his bottom lip.

"There was no need to point a gun at me," he said.

"Point a gun at you? Why, José! Would I want to frighten a loyal servant of Cordoba City Council? Anyway, if I wanted to hurt you I wouldn't need a gun," Anatoli added in a low voice. "I'd simply take you in one hand and squeeze you like a little Spanish grape."

The driver's eyes widened: he believed Lieutenant Grushkov. Come to that, so did I.

"Sit down, my friend," Anatoli went on. "Tell my friend from Moscow what happened on the 29th of March this year."

The driver perched on the edge of a chair and began talking rapidly. Anatoli stopped him from time to time to

29

make things clear for me. Moreno confirmed that he'd been sent to Barajas Airport in Madrid to take Vladimir Alexandrov on a long drive to Cordoba. Then, he added, Anatoli Grushkov had taken his passenger from him and he'd had to drive behind the Soviet car all the way from the airport to the Embassy here. He'd waited half an hour without so much as a cup of coffee being offered to him.

The man was determined to appear hard done by.

"Is that how long Vladimir Alexandrov was in the Embassy? Half an hour?" I asked Anatoli. He nodded.

Moreno said. "But a different man came out of the Embassy to the one who had gone in."

"What do you mean?" I asked in my halting Spanish.

"I mean he had *changed*," the driver emphasized.

"His clothes?"

"No! He came out a very frightened man."

Both he and I stared at my colleague. Anatoli smilingly held up his hands.

"He called Moscow in private," he insisted to me in Russian. "Before we knew it he had rushed out to Señor Moreno's car."

"Who did he speak to in Moscow?" I asked.

"We don't know. But I agree with our friend José, here. There was something about that phone call. Alexandrov was a scared-looking man by the time he left."

I turned back to the driver. "So you took him to Cordoba?"

"No, Señor. Not at once. The gentleman wanted me to take him to a bar."

"He was meeting someone?"

"No, no! He told me to take him to *any* bar. Just get him to the nearest bar. He needed a drink, he said."

"So that's what you did?"

"Of course. He was only in there an hour yet he staggered out again completely drunk. He collapsed in the back of the car and I drove him to Cordoba."

"He said nothing?" I asked.

Moreno shrugged; his mouth twisted down with disgust. "How could he? When he wasn't asleep he was being sick! A five hour journey and I had to drive with a grunting pig in the back of my car! We got to Cordoba at around seven in the evening."

"You took him to the conference?"

"No. I took him to the university where the foreigners were staying. The secretary met him and managed to get him to his room."

"The secretary's name?"

"Señora Ruiz Schrader," he said. "Poor Señora Schrader. She says Señor Alexandrov left his room later that night without telling anyone. The police discovered him later lying unconscious in the street. He must have been drinking again. They took him back to the university. Russians drink like pigs."

Very slowly Anatoli reached inside his jacket and pulled out his automatic pistol. Moreno's mouth fell open and his hands clenched his hat. Anatoli released the ammunition clip, checked that it was loaded and pushed it back in place. Then he took a handkerchief from his pocket and began to polish it lovingly. It lay across his knee but the barrel was pointed at the driver. His voice was very gentle as he said. "You are so right, my dear José. We Russians drink, as you say, like pigs. But, luckily for you, young Yuri and I are not Russians; we are Georgians. So we won't shoot you just yet. In fact, if you co-operate, we won't even tell Moscow what you said."

"You wouldn't dare harm me!" the driver squawked.

31

"Cordoba is run by a Communist Party council. The mayor is a loyal Communist. I am sure if we asked him nicely he would arrange an accident for you... Just to keep Moscow happy."

José Moreno swallowed hard.

"But I have come all the way from Cordoba to help you," he whined.

"So tell us what else happened to Alexandrov!" Anatoli shouted.

CHAPTER NINE

"Señora Schrader," Moreno murmured, "told me that Señor Alexandrov managed to get to the conference for his speech at 10:00 am the next morning. But she told me he spoke strangely. "

"Hangover, no doubt," I said.

Moreno shrugged. "Señora Schrader said he was due to attend a press conference that afternoon but he simply wandered off into town again."

"Drinking?"

"I think so."

Anatoli said to me in Russian: "That's what the authorities in Cordoba said. They phoned us here for advice – asking what they should do about him."

"Bring him back here," I suggested.

"Exactly what I told them," Anatoli grinned.

Looking puzzled, Moreno put in, "Señora Schrader says he got back to the university at 3:00 am. He was trying to pay the taxi driver with a 50 dollar bill."

"You mean a 50 peseta bill," I said.

"No, Señor. Señora Schrader says that was the problem. It was a 50 dollar bill. She paid the driver herself but Señor Alexandrov was too drunk to understand. He just kept trying to pay with the dollars."

"Why would Alexandrov be carrying so much US money?" I asked Anatoli.

"Good question. Moscow would only give him pesetas for a trip to Spain. Still, perhaps an American gave it to him," Anatoli suggested.

"Why?"

"To persuade him to defect? Was that where he was during the hours he was missing? Meeting CIA agents in Cordoba bars? Being offered money to go to the US?"

"But why would the US want him?" I asked. "They'd already denounced his work as unoriginal and out of date."

"Maybe they just wanted to stop him wandering the world spouting the Russian version of Nuclear Winter. After all, it was making the US look like the Evil Empire, not us Soviets."

It wasn't enough to go on. I turned back to the driver. "So you brought Alexandrov back to Madrid. Back here?"

He nodded. "Señora Schrader put another driver in with me... Francisco Delgado... in case there was any trouble."

"And was there?"

Moreno spread his hands. "Señor Alexandrov kept asking us to stop every time he saw a roadside bar. We were under orders. We only stopped so he could use a toilet."

"Let me get this right. This was on the Sunday? Sunday March 31?" I asked.

"Yes, Señor."

"And you arrived when?"

"Some time early in the evening."

"And he was brought here?"

"He kept asking to be taken to the airport. Straight to Barajas Airport, he kept saying."

"He must have known his future was bleak," said Anatoli to me. He made a downward motion with his hand. "The rocket had finally hit the ground."

I agreed. "He'd never leave Moscow again."

"Worse! He'd never work as a scientist again. The last Soviet scientist who made a drunken exhibition of himself ended up with a job as the janitor in a block of flats."

"So why was he in such a hurry to get back to Moscow?" I asked.

Anatoli lowered his head and looked at me seriously from under those thick eyebrows. "Come on, Yuri. You're not that innocent. If he was heading for the airport he was planning to take a flight to anywhere... anywhere but Moscow. And he possessed the US dollars to do it."

"Yes. So it looks as if defection was on his mind early in the evening."

"And by late evening he had disappeared.You do not need a US super-computer to put two and two together, eh, Yuri?"

"His wife won't get any money if we report that, Anatoli."

"But if he was kidnapped? That's one theory."

"Kidnapped by the CIA... or by the KGB?" I asked.

"Or neither," he said. He tucked his gun away in his jacket. "Finish squeezing the juice out of this Spanish grape, and I'll tell you an incredible story."

"Señor Moreno," I said. "You did not take Señor Alexandrov to the airport."

"Certainly not! I had my instructions from Cordoba to bring him here. I always obey instructions."

"Very worthy, I'm sure. And what did he say when you refused?"

"We didn't exactly refuse. We just said, 'Yes we'll take you to the airport' but headed for here instead."

"And when he saw where you were taking him?"

"He went crazy like a bull. He tore at the door handle... but of course it was locked. He ripped the handle off the door. Señor Alexandrov was a strong man. I was afraid he would attack me. He hammered at the glass in the door... but it was the official City Council car. The glass is bulletproof." Suddenly he added. "Your Embassy have still not paid for the repair to our door handle! When the mayor wants to get out of the car I have to walk to the back door and open it."

"The exercise will do the Spanish grape good," I said in Russian to Anatoli. He laughed, Moreno scowled. I turned to the latter.

"What happened when you reached the Embassy?"

"I opened the door for Señor Alexandrov."

"And he walked in here?"

"That *I* can answer," Anatoli interrupted, shaking his head. "He ran off down the road. As I told you, he was a frightened man!"

I stared at my colleague in exasperation. Was there no end to the strange turns this case would take?

Chapter Ten

"Did you run after the Doctor?" I asked Anatoli, looking doubtfully at his bulk.

He wheezed with laughter. "I wouldn't run even if you threw a bomb at me. No, one of the staff caught him and talked him into coming back. We told Moreno here to take him to the hotel we use for guests. The Hotel Habana. The little squirt refused."

I asked Moreno in Spanish. "Why did you refuse to take Señor Alexandrov to the Hotel Habana?"

The little man stuck out that bottom lip again and said, "I was told to bring the Russian here and I brought him here. We are not a taxi service for your Embassy. I wanted to get back to Cordoba. I have a wife and family to think of and…"

"So you refused. Fine. Did you see what happened next?"

"I can answer that, comrade," Anatoli broke in. But Moreno was already answering.

"They threw him into a van. Two great thugs threw him into a van."

"Oh, I'm a thug now, am I?" Anatoli said mildly and moved his hand just a fraction towards the inside of his jacket.

"No, no, Señor… I meant you took the professor away."

"But we didn't force him, did we? We invited him to get into the Embassy van and he got in, didn't he?"

Moreno hesitated a second then said, "Yes, Señor."

"You placed Señor Alexandrov's bags in the back of the van and then you drove off."

"Yes, Señor."

"And now you may drive off back to Cordoba," Anatoli

said, dismissing him.

"The money for my petrol, Señor..."

"Will be paid for by Cordoba City Council, no doubt. If I gave you money you would pocket it and charge the petrol to Cordoba anyway. Am I right?"

Moreno's eyes sparked angrily but they were fixed on the spot on Anatoli's jacket that concealed the gun. He jammed what remained of his hat on his head and stalked out of the room.

The old agent swallowed a glass of vodka as if he was washing the taste of the sour man out of his mouth.

"What's going on, Anatoli? Did that man speak the truth?" I said at last. "Alexandrov came back here and you packed him off to a hotel?"

Anatoli leaned forward. "Listen, Yuri, I'm being straight with you. The Doctor was afraid of something, yes, but what? It might simply have been paranoia. Someone here was out to get him, he thought. He didn't want to stay here and we had no reason to force him. We wanted to show he was free to do as he wished. We took him and his bags to Hotel Habana and made sure he checked in. The last time I saw him he was headed for room 614."

That seemed a curious thing to do when Alexandrov was obviously out of control, and needed monitoring. I didn't comment but let Anatoli go on. "We checked with Moscow and they simply told us to collect him the next morning, April the first, and make sure he took a flight back to Moscow."

"But he'd already gone?"

"I took one of the security men with me and we reached the hotel around 10:00 am. The receptionist rang his room. No answer. She gave us a pass key and we went up. His luggage was all there, but the great man himself had gone.

The receptionist checked with her colleague who'd been on duty the night before. It seems Vladimir Alexandrov had left the hotel at 11:00 pm the night before and returned very late, incredibly drunk. He had tried to get into a gambling place next to the hotel, demanding wine. They refused to let him in so he went back into the hotel to find another way through. He eventually got into the gambling place – and was thrown out again. This time he didn't return."

"What did you do?"

"First we had to keep the hotel happy – clear Alexandrov's luggage from his room and pay the bill. Then we went to the local police and asked if he'd been picked up. They knew nothing about him. He wasn't in their cells and they weren't interested in looking for a lost Russian… the inspector said they had enough lost Spaniards to worry about."

"So he could have run away? Taken a taxi to the airport and jumped on the first flight out?"

"Airport security were no more helpful than the police, but you'd think they'd have noticed a drunk Russian staggering about looking for a plane to catch."

"I meant the airline flight lists. His name would have been on one of the flights out."

Anatoli shook his head. "Not without his passport. It was handed to us later that day. Someone said it had been found in the rubbish bin of his room, someone else that it was lying in a bin *outside* the hotel. The woman who dropped the passport at the Embassy disappeared before I could question her."

I thought about it. "He had a fake passport and identity papers and left with those. That would explain why he dumped his own passport," I guessed.

"No," my colleague said. "If you are planning to defect you do not draw attention to yourself by getting into drunken arguments with gambling parlour attendants – and you do not leave your passport. You take it with you, so the KGB are looking for a man travelling as Vladimir Alexandrov."

"You think he was kidnapped by the CIA?"

"I think he was kidnapped – but not by the CIA," he replied. His eyes were sparkling under the heavy eyebrows. He was teasing me.

"You know something about the CIA involvement?" I asked.

"First I need to know how much I can trust you, my friend. How much will go on your report to the Colonel?"

"The Colonel will want to know why you left Vladimir Alexandrov alone in the hotel – but I can probably explain that away. But I can't be sure what to leave out of the report until I know what should have gone in it, can I?"

Anatoli chuckled. "Very well, Yuri. I can see I'm going to have to take a little risk with you. But, for my sake, there is one thing you must not tell Moscow. They must not know that I break their little rules from time to time. It gets results, but they wouldn't like it."

He pushed himself to his feet, crossed to the wall and pulled a bell rope. "I want you to meet an unofficial contact of mine. A very experienced agent who helps me once in a while."

There was a soft knock on the door and a woman walked in. I guessed she was around 30; her brown hair was cut short and she had a tanned, intelligent face. She was wearing jeans.

"Gillian Smetna," said Anatoli, "meet Yuri Velikhov."

Her handshake was firm and she looked at me with

40

interest. "Pleased to meet you," she said in Russian but with an accent I couldn't quite place.

"You are Lithuanian, perhaps?" I asked.

She laughed and showed her fine, white teeth. "No. American!"

"An American!"

"A *bona fide* American – born in Florida," she smiled.

"Brilliant!" I said to Anatoli. "Getting a genuine American to work for the KGB!"

Now it was Anatoli's turn to laugh. "Will you tell him, Gillian, or shall I?"

"Don't tease him," she said. She looked me in the eye and said, "I work in the American Embassy here in Madrid. But I'm not a KGB 'plant'. I'm a one hundred per cent loyal American. And I work for the CIA."

Luckily the sofa was behind me; I felt my knees fold and I sat down.

I was face to face with the Enemy.

Chapter Eleven

Anatoli burst into laughter; Gillian Smetna looked at him reprovingly. She sat down opposite me.

"Anatoli must have his little joke," she said. "Sometimes I think he's just a great big kid. You see, Mr Velikhov, our governments keep secrets from one another, and it's our job to protect those secrets. But there are *some* cases where it pays for us to co-operate. There's no need for Anatoli to creep round trying to find out what happened to someone like Doctor Alexandrov. He's too fat to creep around anyway." She patted his paunch affectionately.

Anatoli pulled a face. "We co-operate on things like *this*. When Alexandrov disappeared I simply went straight to Gillian and asked, 'Have you got him?'"

"And have you?" I asked Miss Smetna.

"I'll tell you what I told Anatoli," she replied. "Why would we *want* him? He was not a scientist any longer, he was a travelling Nuclear Winter show. We believe he was wrong about Nuclear Winter and his reputation was disappearing faster than an ice cream in the Spanish Sun."

"So what *did* happen to him?"

"I believe he was kidnapped, but not by the KGB, and not by the CIA. By MI5."

"The British Secret Service!" I cried. "Why?"

"It's their style. They do that kind of thing more often than us. Maybe they even thought they were doing us a favour."

"So where is he now?"

"The fact that he hasn't shown up is bad news," she admitted. "It's possible the British were a bit too rough

42

and he died. Of course that would explain why his body was never found. They are also pretty expert at disposing of that kind of problem."

My mind was racing and I began to draw a picture of Alexandrov's fate.

"That's certainly an amazing story," I said. "It sounds like a reasonable explanation. The KGB had no reason to kidnap Alexandrov, though he may have been something of an embarrassment. The CIA had no reason to kidnap him, though the Nuclear Winter theory showed them in a bad light, what with their massive arms build-up. No body or trace of him has been found by the Spanish police, so it's unlikely – though still possible – that he was mugged in a bar somewhere by local bandits. Therefore, the solution can only be MI5. They came over to Spain and without so much as a hint to their closest allies, the CIA, snatched a perfectly decent, if rather drunk, Russian scientist out of his hotel bedroom. Brilliant."

Miss Smetna and Anatoli looked at each other rather uncomfortably, it seemed to me.

"Yuri. Please listen to me," said Anatoli after a pause. He went and sank into a chair. "As you well know, our country is going through a most important phase of its development. What Comrade Gorbachev is trying to do is nothing less than revolutionary. He is trying to make us see that our old ways, the ways of Stalin, Brezhnev and the rest – the policies of oppression – simply will not do if we are to compete with the West. We tried to beat them in a nuclear arms race. The effort has, I am afraid to say, failed. You look shocked. But I think you know it's true..."

"What has all this to with Alexandrov?" I said.

"Well, nothing directly. It's more a question of political

atmosphere. In the old days, KGB would have tracked down Alexandrov at all costs and had him eliminated. That is, if he defected. Today that seems somehow out of place – even to an old KGB hand like me. The so-called secrets Alexandrov might have given to the West can no longer be considered, shall we say, vital. But perhaps I have just become too soft on the West..."

Anatoli smiled at Miss Smetna, who smiled back.

"Are you saying that you have further information about Alexandrov, but that you do not choose to tell me?" I asked him.

There was a silence. Anatoli looked at me steadily, as though defying me to think the worst. Then he said:

"No Yuri. I am saying that my attitude to many things has changed. I am also saying that I have done as much as I can to find our Nuclear Winter Man. If you choose to think that I have not done my job or that I was involved in some way in Alexandrov's disappearance, then so be it. How you report back to Moscow must be your decision."

I sat there uncertain of what to think. I looked from Anatoli to the American woman, then back to Anatoli. He was as good as putting his life in my hands. He must have guessed the orders I had should I find he'd been disloyal in any way.

I also had the impression there was some arrangement between him and the girl – some kind of understanding.

"The Colonel," I said deliberately, "is sure to be quite satisfied with what I have to report."

Chapter Twelve

"So, what did happen to our Doctor Alexandrov?" the Colonel asked, sitting back with his hands clasped over his stomach.

"The CIA helped Vladimir Alexandrov to disappear," I said, looking down at that carpet of his again.

"Have you any evidence?" he asked.

"None. They are too clever to leave a trail."

"Then why are you so sure they're responsible?"

"Because they are trying too hard to persuade us that they did *not* do it. They used a CIA agent, Gillian Smetna, to infiltrate our Embassy in Madrid. A persuasive woman, Miss Smetna. She made friends with Comrade Grushkov, convincing him that the British were responsible for kidnapping Alexandrov."

"You are sure Grushkov swallowed her story?"

"Oh, yes. He produced her like some trump card to prove his cleverness," I said. "But my father had an old Georgian saying: 'The old bear falls into the old trap'."

The Colonel stared at me.

"He was not so clever, then," he said.

"No – he was a traitor. He decided he wanted the best of both worlds – an easy life in the West working in partnership with the CIA. Who knows, he may even have been a double agent. At the very least, the Americans took advantage of his weakness, planting false information on him which he faithfully relayed back to Moscow. Like the lies he told about the British kidnapping Alexandrov."

"We suspected old Grushkov for a long while," the Colonel said quietly.

"You didn't tell me."

"No doubt you liked the man?" he said, ignoring my remark.

"I did."

"I liked him too. He and I used to be friends of a kind. But that was long ago. I'm sure he asked you to keep quiet about his little secrets?"

"He did."

"If you *had* done then we would have found out sooner or later. We would have had to deal with you most severely," he said. His voice was toneless; killing and human pain were simply matters of bureaucratic record. He sat forward and shifted through the pile of forms on his desk. "I see you have returned the clothes and accounted for every rouble you spent."

"Yes, comrade."

"Good, good. You may yet make a reasonable agent, Velikhov. You may even go all the way to the top. I'd better look out for my job."

That was his idea of a joke.

"Only one thing you failed to bring back," he went on, looking at the yellow armaments form.

"A single bullet," I said.

"Only one?" he said in wonder. "I'd have thought it would have taken more than one, somehow. Grushkov was quite a bull."

"I've been well trained," I said. "And you can be sure the body will never be found."

"So you are both loyal *and* discreet," he said with a grim smile. "Excellent, excellent. Unlike Doctor Alexandrov – a careless and a foolish man. I think he was beginning to believe that US nonsense about us being the evil enemy."

"And his wife and daughter?" I asked.

46

"They will have his pay sent to them again. That will make it appear we are happy about his defection."

I nodded. "That way the CIA will be confused. They will wonder if he was in fact planted by us. Clever."

The Colonel got up and looked out the window towards the Academy of Science.

"Velikhov, I can't help thinking the good Doctor was right about one thing – a nuclear war is unwinnable. The consequences would be catastrophic for all sides. That much we know. However, what we know and how we behave are, of course, two different things: that is politics. From that point of view Alexandrov was dangerous. He was an idealist. The Americans can keep him."

An hour later, using a telephone line I knew to be secure, I dialled a number in Europe. A gruff, familiar voice answered. I said:

"The Colonel swallowed it. You're officially dead. But you were right – he always suspected you."

Anatoli's chuckle rolled down the line. "Thank you, Yuri. Now that I'm dead I feel so much better! The new Soviet Union belongs to the likes of you. I feel I'm leaving it in safe hands."

"Good luck, Anatoli," I said. "Enjoy America."

"I will," he promised. "I will."

Glossary

CIA
(CENTRAL INTELLIGENCE AGENCY)
US agency set up in the late 1940s to protect the government from hostile foreign nations. The CIA employs agents in over 150 countries to send back information which it then assesses, offering its analysis to other US agencies. The CIA also attempts to prevent any risk to the national security posed by foreign spies.

GLASNOST
A policy of 'openness' instituted by Soviet premier Mikhail Gorbachev in the late 1980s. After some 50 years of tyranny and oppression, the idea of *glasnost* was to encourage a limited amount of free expression among Soviet peoples.

KGB
A government agency of the former Soviet Union. The letters 'KGB' are an abbreviation of the Russian words meaning 'Committee for State Security'. The KGB's main function was to ensure that the Communist Party kept control of the Soviet Union. It operated a secret police force, and was also involved with gathering information about other

countries. Another important role of the KGB was secretly to aid foreign governments or other organizations that it considered sympathetic to the Soviet Union. The KGB was disbanded in 1991 when the Soviet Union was dissolved.

THE KREMLIN
A 'fortified enclosure' in the centre of Moscow that became a seat of government as early as the 1100s. This vast aggregation of palaces, walls and towers was the centre of czarist (monarchist) rule from the mid-1500s until 1712, when Peter the Great moved the Russian capital to St Petersburg. However, with the Communist Revolution of 1917, government offices were moved back to the Kremlin, and today it forms the heart of a democratic Russia.

MI5
(MILITARY INTELLIGENCE 5)
Branch of the British Secret Services heavily involved in the fight against Communism during the Cold War. The service scored some notable successes against its Communist opponents, encouraging the defection of a number of high-ranking Russian and East European officials. However, the organization was itself rocked by spy scandals in the 1960s

and 70s.

NUCLEAR WINTER
This refers to the potentially catastrophic impact a nuclear war could have on our environment. The fall-out from a nuclear holocaust could cause disastrous changes to the Earth's atmosphere and climate. If large amounts of smoke from fires spread and covered parts of the Earth, then sunlight would not be able to reach the ground. With less sunlight, reduced temperatures and less rain, we would struggle to survive.

STRATOSPHERE
The upper portion of the Earth's atmosphere beginning approximately 11km above the Earth's surface and extending to approximately 50km above it. Here temperatures are stable and clouds are rare.

50

BIOGRAPHIES

This story contains fictional characters and investigates a true-life mystery. Before you look at the facts and make up your own mind, here's a brief biography of some of the characters mentioned in the story:

VLADIMIR VALENTINOVICH ALEXANDROV (ACTUAL CHARACTER)

Renowned Russian scientist who travelled the world investigating and relating his Nuclear Winter theory. A popular and sociable man, his disappearance at the age of forty-seven has never been adequately explained.

ALYA & OLGA ALEXANDROV (ACTUAL CHARACTERS)

The wife and daughter of Vladimir Alexandrov. The Doctor seemed devoted to them, smuggling drugs into Russia to alleviate Alya's liver condition, and smuggling tissue samples out of the country for doctors in England to analyze and possibly treat. Both mother and daughter were desperately unhappy at Alexandrov's disappearance and wrote to US and Soviet authorities in an unsuccessful attempt to track him down.

YURI VELIKHOV – NARRATOR
(FICTIONAL CHARACTER)
A young KGB officer assigned to trace Vladimir Alexandrov. The Soviets *did* actually assign someone to investigate the scientist's disappearance and this would seem to suggest that they had nothing to do with it.

ANATOLI GRUSHKOV
(ACTUAL CHARACTER, DISGUISED NAME)
The KGB officer posted in the Soviet Union's Madrid Embassy. Embassy officials such as Grushkov were supposed to be working to help Soviet citizens in Spain. In fact some of them were KGB agents, gathering information and performing acts of espionage when ordered to do so by Moscow headquarters. Grushkov sent Vladimir Alexandrov to the Habana hotel – possibly against the scientist's will. The next day Grushkov had Alexandrov's room cleared of his possessions and had any clues to his disappearance removed.

THE COLONEL
(FICTIONAL CHARACTER)
Part of the KGB's high command, his responsibilities would have involved directing operatives on cases of high sensitivity both at home and abroad.

JOSÉ MORENO
(ACTUAL CHARACTER – DISGUISED NAME)

Driver for Cordoba City Council. Gave evidence as to Vladimir Alexandrov's behaviour from the time he arrived in Spain. Later the Spanish refused to give Moreno's address or contact number to investigators. They also denied that some parts of his story were true. They said, for example, that Moreno was wrong to say a terrified Alexandrov tore the door handle off in an attempt to escape the Soviet Embassy staff – the Spaniards claim that the scientist simply pulled an ashtray out of the door when he grasped the wrong handle.

GILLIAN SMETNA
(FICTIONAL CHARACTER)

CIA agent posted at the US Embassy in Madrid. Like Anatoli Grushkov, to all outward appearances she would be working as an Embassy official; in fact this was simply a 'cover' for espionage. The CIA did have agents in Madrid at the time of Alexandrov's disappearance, and would have had the necessary skills to help him defect to the USA – if he'd asked. He would certainly have found it difficult to defect without such help because he would have needed a new passport, new identity, money and 'sponsors' to get him into America.

CLASSIFIED FILES

The problem in solving the case of Vladimir Alexandrov is that there are several plausible explanations for his disappearance. You must use your own judgement, and the evidence available, to make up your mind as to which is *the most likely*.

Here are some of the possible theories of what could have taken place...

Defection to USA

Vladimir Alexandrov was fairly happy living and working in the USSR, but his success was not very well rewarded. He enjoyed fine food, good clothes and luxurious holidays. When he met US scientists in the Soviet Union the first thing he did was arrange to get himself invited to their country. They were happy to invite him. They wanted to show that even if their governments were at each other's throats, scientists were above politics. The world's scientific community felt that it could exist peacefully and co-operate. Alexandrov enjoyed his first visit to the US – he felt comfortable in the comparatively wealthy and free lifestyle of the West. Even the work was more rewarding with the access he enjoyed to super-powerful American computer technology. Alexandrov's wife went on one visit with him and saw for herself how good life was in the US. He decided to defect, but he realized that if he did it openly then the KGB would come after him. Instead, the scientist simply had to 'disappear' and emerge in the US with a new identity.

BUT...

Why did Alexandrov arouse suspicion by making a drunken display of himself in Madrid? This would only have drawn attention to himself – quite the opposite of discreet defection. It also seems bizarre that a family-loving man like Alexandrov would desert his wife and daughter. Mrs Alexandrov had long been suffering a serious liver complaint, and their child Olga had severe asthma. Could the scientist really have *chosen* to leave such a vulnerable family behind him, knowing their income might be cut off if his defection was discovered?

Defection to Spain

When an article appeared in a US magazine criticizing his work on Nuclear Winter, Alexandrov perhaps felt that he could not return to Russia. He knew that when he went back to Moscow he would be in disgrace. His apartment would be taken away from him and he'd end up with a low-paid job in a third rate flat. His wife and daughter would have to suffer this disgrace with him, and their lower standard of living would undoubtedly damage the health of both his wife and daughter. Vladimir Alexandrov was miserable and drank heavily while he worked out what to do. Then, full of Spanish wine, he made a decision on the spur of the moment. He would simply walk away from his hotel room, leave all his belongings and passport behind, and ask the Spanish if he could stay in their country. This is supported by the curious behaviour of the Spanish. At first they co-operated with investigators looking for the scientist; once they realized Alexandrov had defected to *them,* they had to revise some of their stories. José Moreno was suddenly no longer available for interview for outside investigators, and the Spanish said that their earlier stories of a damaged car were exaggerated. They did not want the case fully investigated because *they* had engineered his defection.

BUT...

While the Russians stated that the Spanish were not trying to solve the mystery, they never accused them of being involved. Moreover, the Spanish would upset the world's most powerful nations, the USSR and the USA, if any involvement was discovered. That would damage Spanish trade – hardly worth while for a man who can have been of little political value to them.

KGB Kidnap
Alexandrov was an embarrassment to the Soviet Union authorities. They had read US criticism of his work: Soviet science was made to look old-fashioned and even incompetent. Alexandrov was also accused by American scientists of saying just what Russian politicians wanted him to: he wasn't a scientist – he was a mouthpiece for Russian propaganda. By the time of the Cordoba conference he had been discredited, and was of no further use to his government. Moreover, when he started drinking and was found unconscious on the streets of Cordoba, he was doing the reputation of the Soviet Union a great deal of harm. He had to be safely collected by the KGB and transported back to the Soviet Union. He was followed to the Madrid gambling parlour, grabbed from the street and bundled into a car. The Spanish police stated that the Soviet Union put no pressure on them to find their missing scientist. Is that because the Russians already knew where he was?

BUT...

The Soviet authorities stopped Alexandrov's pay and removed his name from Nuclear Winter publications – probably because they thought of him as a traitor. It's unlikely they would do that if they knew for certain that Alexandrov was *not* a traitor.

CIA kidnap
Alexandrov was working for the cause of peace. He would do anything to encourage the super-powers to give up their nuclear weapons. He painted the bleakest picture of Nuclear Winter imaginable – worse than that envisaged by US scientists. Of course this did not make him popular with those making a living from building and operating those weapons – the US military. They decided to force the Soviet scientist to change his mind. They would kidnap him, take him back to the USA and 'brainwash' him. When they had drugged and intimidated him sufficiently, he would be made to appear in public and go back on his opinions about the probable effects of a nuclear conflict. The CIA couldn't kidnap him in the USA – too much suspicion would be aroused. However, if he went 'missing' in Spain it would look as though he had defected to the USA of his own free will. So CIA agents followed him on his drunken rounds of Madrid, snatched him off the street and concealed him in the US Embassy in Madrid.

BUT...

This represents probably the ultimate conspiracy theory where Alexandrov is concerned. It is easily disproved: the scientist never appeared *anywhere* again to say he was wrong about Nuclear Winter.

MI5 kidnap

An American journalist who investigated the kidnap came up with the theory that the British Secret Service branch MI5 kidnapped Vladimir Alexandrov. Apparently, they did this as a favour to the CIA. The idea was that the CIA would make the Soviet scientist change his Nuclear Winter theory.

BUT...

The source of this information has never been given and cannot be verified. Such an operation could not be carried out without permission from the British Government. Mrs Margaret Thatcher was British Prime Minister at the time and eager to make friends with the new Soviet President Gorbachev. Would she approve a plan by her Secret Service to kidnap a Soviet scientist? If the plot went wrong, and British involvement was uncovered, then relationships between the two countries would be ruined.

Murder

Alexandrov could have been kidnapped by the CIA and drugged to make him talk. However, the operation went badly wrong: he died under the drugs. Alternatively, he might have been assassinated by the KGB. Lastly, he might have been mugged by street criminals, or snatched by Spanish kidnappers and held to ransom. When the Soviet authorities refused to pay the ransom, he was murdered.

BUT...

Spanish police never had any indication that Alexandrov was a victim of crime. He certainly wasn't kidnapped – no kidnap message was ever received. The possibility that he died under CIA questioning seems remote: it was never reported that Alexandrov possessed secrets so vital that the CIA would resort to such drastic measures. As for the KGB assassination theory, this also seems unlikely – especially as they despatched an investigator to Spain to find out what happened to Alexandrov!

Death by natural causes

Vladimir Alexandrov's life was falling apart. After two years of fame, he was out of favour in the scientific community. The recognition he desired at the Soviet Academy of Sciences seemed more and more unattainable. He began drinking to escape his problems. In a drunken stupor he was thrown out of the gambling parlour and wandered through the streets of Madrid. A number of things might have happened to him after that – none of them criminal. He might have taken a taxi in an attempt to reach the airport; if he'd been sick in the taxi, as he was in the Cordoba Council car, the taxi driver may have thrown him out onto the road where he wandered into fields, miles from anywhere. There he might have fallen down a ravine or suffered a heart attack. More simply, however, Alexandrov could have fallen into a river and drowned; his body may have been washed ashore at some quiet spot. People do go missing and their remains are found only many years later.

BUT...

The bodies of people who die of natural causes – unless they die at sea – are generally recovered in some form or another. Alexandrov disappeared over ten years ago and not a single trace of his remains has yet been found.

Alive and well

Alexandrov was a perceptive man. He realized that there was no future for him in Moscow, so he resolved to start a new life in the West. He had a passport forged and adopted a new name. He began behaving oddly to confuse the KGB. On the night of his disappearance, he pretended to be drunk and incapable of going anywhere. He deliberately made a nuisance of himself in the gambling parlour so the attendants would remember him as the Russian too drunk to look after himself. Then he simply collected his false passport and disappeared into the night. With such a passport he could have taken a ship or plane to any destination in the world. He

61

had plenty of money (possibly saved in US dollars) and could find a job in any large city using his computer skills. He spoke English and Italian well, which would have facilitated his assimilation into a number of countries. Sadly, his wife and daughter would have to be abandoned. He calculated, however, that so long as he didn't appear to be a traitor, his family would be looked after in the Soviet Union.

BUT...

It seems strange that his family had no hint whatsoever of such an intention. Also, if he had been ingenious enough to engineer his own disappearance, surely he could arrange for his family to follow him to the West at some later stage? He could also let them know, at the very least, that he was still alive — instead of letting them live on in uncertainty.

NUCLEAR WINTER

For the two years before his disappearance, Doctor Alexandrov's life and work centred on the idea of Nuclear Winter. But were his theories correct? And did they actually have any bearing on his disappearance? Here are a number of facts relating to nuclear war and to Nuclear Winter generally.

Did you know?

1 The Earth's atmosphere is extremely fragile – it's only 0.1 per cent of the diameter of the planet itself. If the Earth were a balloon and you painted it with a coat of varnish, the atmosphere would be equivalent to the thickness of that varnish.

2 In the 1990s, the idea of a Nuclear Winter became less worrying as the threat of nuclear war receded. Instead, environmentalists became more concerned about the destruction of the ozone layer and about the greenhouse warming effect. In fact, the research on Nuclear Winter done in the 1980s provided vital information for later studies on the

63

depletion of the ozone layer and on the greenhouse effect.

3 World War II ended with atomic bombs having been used as military weapons for the first time. Since then, scientists have found ways of packing ten or more nuclear warheads into a single missile. Each warhead can destroy a city. One nuclear submarine can carry enough missiles to destroy 200 cities.

4 The average temperature of the Earth, day and night, in all seasons and all places, is 13 degrees centigrade. If that temperature dropped just three degrees because of a nuclear dust cloud, then disaster would ensue for farmers and food producers: millions would starve. Doctor Alexandrov argued that the fall in average temperature would be far greater than what the American scientists believed. No one could survive such conditions, he claimed.

5 Alexandrov said that, in the event of a nuclear war, his computers predicted something catastrophic: there would be a rise in temperatures on the Tibetan Plateau. In October 1983, he said this rise would cause the mountain snow and mountain glaciers to melt. It would probably result in floods of continental size. Nuclear shelters would therefore no longer protect life on Earth. Unfortunately, Alexandrov could not give the reason for this temperature rise – and none of the US computers agreed with him. This was one of several differences between US and Russian calculations concerning the effects of Nuclear Winter.

6 A greenhouse lets in the light of the Sun, then traps it as heat. The gases in our atmosphere work the same way. If we had no carbon-dioxide in the atmosphere, the temperature of the Earth's surface would fall to at least -20 degrees centigrade! The seas would be frozen; all life would cease to exist. In the event of a nuclear war, the heat from the Sun would not penetrate through to the Earth in the first place. The smoke, soot and dust thrown up by the explosions and fall-out would prevent sunlight entering the atmosphere: Nuclear Winter would ensue.

7 One of the layers of gas lying over the Earth is called the ozone layer. This soaks up ultra-violet light from the Sun – light which can be fatal to humans in large doses. Man has already damaged the ozone layer by producing gases called chlorofluorocarbons (CFCs). Nuclear war, however, would have a still more devastating effect on ozone; survivors who left their shelters would have to face exposure to near-pure ultra-violet light.

8 Scientists have been forced to speculate about what would happen in the event of a Nuclear Winter. Computers have been used to calculate possible effects; however, no computer is big enough to be fed all the possible factors. All calculations obviously depend on the facts fed in at the outset. Alexandrov fed fewer facts into his basic computer than the US scientists did into theirs – so it is likely less accurate results were produced.

9 The cooling effect on the Earth of the nuclear smoke cloud is not the only problem to be faced in a nuclear war, of course. The initial blast would kill millions, and the smoke itself probably choke thousands more. Radiation 'fall-out' would also prove lethal – though its effects would be more gradual. The most dangerous rays – gamma rays – can pass through 30 cm of concrete; on the human body radiation results in poisoning, leading to cancer.

10 Earth has suffered many disastrous natural winters in the past. In 1973, scientists concluded that millions of years ago a comet the size of a small mountain collided with the Earth and caused a huge dust cloud to blot out the Sun. Plants and animals – including the dinosaurs – died *en masse*; it is calculated that around 75 per cent of all species of life disappeared at that time. Earth life recovered and produced a strange species that is capable of going one better and destroying itself: Man. In 1961, US President John Kennedy said, **"Mankind must put an end to war or war will put an end to mankind."**

Vladimir Alexandrov was at the centre of world research into the effects of nuclear war, and clearly believed that the world should be told about these effects. He was eager to persuade world leaders that nuclear war would lead to Nuclear Winter, and that disaster would ensue even for the 'winners'. But how far did he go to persuade people? Did he exaggerate the effects of the great freeze, for example?

If Alexandrov's research concerning the 'great cold' – that it would freeze the oceans and destroy most species – was credible, it would be a powerful argument against the continuing build-up of nuclear weapons in both the USA and the Soviet Union. Certain vested interests in both countries might have found these views unpalatable – even to the extent of killing the man who propounded them.

SECRET SERVICES

The government of any country might use its secret services to deal with a 'problem' such as a troublesome scientist. But how likely was it that one had a hand in Vladimir Alexandrov's disappearance? To help you decide, here is an overview of the world's major secret services.

SOVIET SECRET SERVICES

The KGB behaved in the same way as the CIA. Both were engaged in foreign intelligence and counterintelligence. However, until the disintegration of the Soviet Union the KGB was also functioning as an internal secret police. It carried out surveillance on Soviet Union citizens suspected of being disloyal to the state.

KGB

Full title: Komitet Gosudarstvennoy Bezopasnosti (Committee for State Security)

Roles: The KGB was responsible for...

 Defending the Soviet people against internal and foreign enemies.

68

Watching the Soviet citizens to ensure loyalty, using networks of secret informers controlled by KGB agents.

 Suppression of anti-Soviet behaviour using interrogation, and detention of security 'risks' in prisons, forced labour camps, or psychiatric hospitals.

 Supervision of the political loyalty of the armed forces.

 Control of the Border Guard.

 The KGB worked in close association with the Ministry of Internal Affairs (MVD), which controlled the regular police, the prisons, and the forced labour camps.

Outside the Soviet Union, the KGB's main tasks were espionage, counter-espionage and the carrying-out of operations which would increase Soviet power in other countries.

69

History

The KGB was set up in 1954 to take over the role of a series of security agencies that had existed in the Soviet Union since the Revolution. These were the Cheka (1917-22), the OGPU (1923-34), the GUGB (1934-41), the NKGB (1941-46), the MGB (1946-53), and the MVD (1953-54).

The KGB were immensely powerful; they took their orders directly from the President and could act outside the law. Kidnapping, imprisoning or eliminating 'subversives' would be a normal day's work for KGB agents.

One of the directors of the KGB was Yuri V. Andropov. Like Gorbachev after him, he showed the power of the organization when he went on to become Soviet President. He died in 1982, shortly before the problems of Nuclear Winter were raised.

In 1991, the Soviet Union broke up into a series of independent states and the KGB was disbanded. However, it is certain that these states – especially the Russian state – have their new forms of secret service.

70

US SECRET SERVICES

The United States of America has two organizations to deal with state secrets. The CIA, which gathers and collates intelligence, and the Federal Bureau of Investigation (FBI), which ensures that US secrets remain secure. Naturally, these organizations often work together, and both were interested in Vladimir Alexandrov's activities.

CIA

Full title: Central Intelligence Agency
Roles: The CIA is responsible for...

 Gathering secret information concerning matters of national security.

 Keeping the US government informed of foreign activities that affect the country.

 Supporting US combat forces by providing information on the enemy forces.

 Involving themselves in the politics and economics of foreign countries to help US interests.

 Preventing foreign agents from 'penetrating' secret US organizations.

History

The CIA was formed in 1947, and was actively involved in subversive operations abroad. This went disastrously wrong in 1961, when the CIA provided training and equipment for a group of Cubans to invade their homeland, now governed by Communists under Fidel Castro. The failure of this invasion, known as the Bay of Pigs, almost involved the USA in a full-scale war with Cuba.

The CIA was reorganized by President John Kennedy, but a 1975 investigation by the US Congress found that it had been involved in illegal plots such as the attempted assassination of foreigners abroad. The organization was placed in the control of elected members of Congress; unlike the KGB, it was answerable to the American people – in theory! But in 1986, a year after the disappearance of Alexandrov, it was again in trouble for meddling in Iranian affairs and in Nicaraguan civil war.

The CIA's partners, the FBI, questioned US scientists about Vladimir Alexandrov on April 3, 1985 – two days after he disappeared. They wanted to know if the scientist was interested in defection to America. It was clear FBI agents knew nothing about Alexandrov's disappearance! Does this imply that the CIA could be responsible for Alexandrov's disappearance,

but were slow to tell their FBI colleagues?
Or does it mean simply that the Americans
were not involved at all?

BRITISH SECRET SERVICES
The British system is under the control of
the Prime Minister and his cabinet. Like the
US system it is divided into two sections –
MI6 and MI5. The latter is the best-known,
an intelligence organization now working in
association with the British police
department known as 'Special Branch'. The
responsibilities of MI6, however, are roughly
equivalent to those of the CIA.

MI5
Full title: Military Intelligence Department 5
Roles: MI5 is responsible for. . .

 Anti-terrorist activity

 Defence

 Serious crime

History
This branch of the British Secret Services
was involved in fighting Communism during
the Cold War, and engineered the defection
from the former USSR of important scientists
and officials to the West. The careful guard
that was kept over its activities was
recently relaxed a little when the British

government demanded it become more accountable to Parliament.

MI5 hit the news in a blaze of publicity in 1992 when Stella Rimington became its Director-General, the first woman ever to head a branch of the British Secret Services.

MI6
Full title: Military Intelligence Department 6
Roles: MI6 is responsible for...

 Espionage

 Counter-espionage

 Overseas action

History
The British Government finally admitted the existence of the organization in 1992. Colin McColl was named as its head, and in 1994 he was succeeded by David Spedding. It became more open to public inquiry; it was revealed that the headquarters were based at Vauxhall Cross in London. Its activities, and the money it spent, were to be made known to Members of the British Parliament.

Alexandrov visited Britain on his travels, asking British medical experts to examine his wife's tissue samples. There is no doubt MI6 would have watched him carefully; however, there is little evidence that MI6 was involved in his disappearance.

THE COLD WAR

The phrase 'Cold War' was coined by US journalist Walter Lippmann, who wrote a book about the long-standing tensions between the USA and the USSR.

The two nations had been hostile to each other since 1917, when the Communists seized power from the Czar. The US did not recognize the Communist USSR until 1933.

In 1939, an alliance was forged between the two nations to defeat Adolf Hitler's Germany. But as soon as the war ended in 1945, the USSR moved quickly to turn Eastern European countries into Communist states.

In the stand-off that ensued, the USA had one great advantage – nuclear weapons. While the Americans remained the sole nuclear power, the USSR would not dare to attack Western Europe.

However, in the early 1950s the Russians began to create their own nuclear weapons. Both superpowers then raced to create huge nuclear stockpiles. Tensions rose; only the 'balance of terror' prevented outright nuclear war.

Nevertheless, nuclear war did come close on a number of occasions in the period following World War II. In 1962, Communist Cuba declared that it was about to station Russian nuclear weapons there – in America's 'back yard'. The USA was furious; there was no way they could allow foreign nuclear weapons to be so close to American soil.

President Kennedy threatened nuclear war if the Russians dared to do this. Eventually, the Soviet Union backed down, and the Cuban Missile Crisis was resolved. However, throughout the 1960s and 70s each nation went on to build still more deadly weapons.

A turning point of kinds was reached in 1983, when President Reagan announced the creation of a Star Wars defence system: Soviet missiles, he claimed, could be shot down by laser-cannon mounted in satellites. He implied that the United States was once again in the lead and that the Soviet Union could not possibly win a nuclear war.

The Soviet Union, bankrupted by its disastrous involvement in the Afghan War, realized that it did simply not have the resources to compete with US technology. With the election of Mikhail Gorbachev as President, Soviet foreign policy underwent a drastic change: agreement was reached with the USA to slow down the nuclear arms race, and relations with the West thawed.

The Cold War ended in 1991 with the break-up of the USSR. The threat of nuclear war, however, has not disappeared entirely. One of the sovereign states in the former Soviet Union might elect an unstable leader, who might just be inclined to brandish his nuclear stockpiles at an enemy. The USA, too, has to be sure to tread carefully in its foreign policy, avoiding such a crisis as occurred in Cuba.

NUCLEAR WEAPONS

So what are these nuclear weapons that Vladimir Alexandrov was warning us about?

The smallest particle of matter is an atom. The mathematician Albert Einstein calculated that if you split an atom it would give off a tremendous amount of energy. Scientists started experimenting to see if Einstein was correct. An Italian-born scientist, living in America, succeeded in 1934. His name was Enrico Fermi.

But controlling the explosion of an atom is difficult. The explosion will make other atoms explode which in turn will make other atoms explode and so on. With a small starting explosion you can create a hugely destructive device. A sphere the size of a tennis ball could explode with the same force as *twenty thousand* tons of TNT (high explosive). With this knowledge, the idea of developing an atomic weapon was born.

During World War II, a race developed between the United States and Germany to develop the first atomic bomb. Germany already had the V1 and V2 rockets which it used in an attempt to bomb Britain into submission. If German planes had carried atomic bombs then London and its inhabitants would have been obliterated.

But the US won the race to become the

first atomic nation. Germany was defeated by sheer force but Japan refused to surrender. The US decided to use the world's first atomic weapons to flatten two Japanese cities – Hiroshima and Nagasaki. There was no way Japan could win a war against such terrible weapons and the Japanese gave in.

Those bombs didn't just kill with the blast – deadly black rain containing radioactive 'fall-out' fell from the skies onto the survivors. The black rain caused horrific burns. The air was contaminated and those that survived the initial blast died slower, even more painful deaths caused by the 'fall-out'.

In 1949 the Soviet Union exploded its own atomic weapon and the US no longer held the power of war and peace.

By 1952 a Hydrogen bomb was created that was a thousand times more powerful than an atomic bomb – in fact it used an atomic bomb as a trigger just to set it off. Bombs could now do as much damage as a *million* tons of TNT.

The temperature generated inside a Hydrogen bomb in the instant before it explodes rises to tens of millions of degrees.

Hydrogen bombs were tested in order to assess the damage they could do. At first scientists thought they'd be studying the effects of blast and heat...

Blast

The sudden explosion produces a shock wave that moves outwards from the bomb. It creates a wind much stronger than any hurricane and, like a hurricane, will flatten structures that stand in its way. People in the open will be thrown at high speed – until they hit something solid and are crushed – or they will be trapped under falling buildings if they are indoors.

Heat

The extreme temperatures inside a nuclear bomb will create a ball of flaming gas called a fireball – this would be as much as 5km across. People in the open will be burned and buildings will catch fire. But people 30km away will be burned by something called thermal radiation. Under some conditions the fires can create a firestorm – an updraught whereby winds are drawn into the centre. Dust and ash and soot are carried high into the atmosphere. This happened at Hiroshima but not at Nagasaki.

Radiation

Scientists involved in these tests had not anticipated the high levels of radiation. Radioactive fall-out was far worse than anyone had imagined. The pollution or 'fall-out' from the bombs went on killing long after the blast and the fires were gone. This nuclear radiation – unlike the thermal radiation – doesn't just touch the skin and pass on. It penetrates deep into the body in much the same way x-rays do. These 'gamma' rays can cause serious injury. Radiation poisoning is one of the most dangerous effects of nuclear bombing because winds can carry radiation clouds over vast areas.

Once the effects of fall-out on this scale were discovered scientists began to build 'clean' nuclear bombs called 'fusion' bombs. The radiation from a fusion bomb could do serious damage to military personnel on a battlefield – penetrating tanks and armoured vehicles to kill the soldiers – but it would not spread much beyond the battlefield to kill innocent civilians or damage property a few kilometres away.

Climate
But it was another 30 years before scientists voiced their concern about the effects of a Nuclear Winter. When they did, they stated that even if the US and USSR used less than half of their nuclear store of weapons the Earth's climate would change. They stressed the difficulty of accurately assessing the long term effects. While blast, heat and radiation damage had all been seen and measured, Nuclear Winter can only be seen and measured if vast quantities of nuclear weapons are exploded... and no one

is going to do that just to test the theory of Nuclear Winter! As a result some people refused to accept that a Nuclear Winter would occur. The US Department of Defence released a statement in 1985 which said it accepted most of the Nuclear Winter calculations... but this would not affect its defence policies!

Albert Einstein, the great mind behind the development of nuclear power, died in 1955. One of the last things he wrote before his death indicated a sad but resigned understanding of the consequences of his calculations. He wrote, **"The conflict today is no more than an old style struggle for power. The difference is that, this time, both parties know that should the quarrel deteriorate into actual war, mankind is doomed."**

It was and is up to scientists to ensure that the defence departments of every country in the world understand the potential disaster of a full scale nuclear war.

Vladimir Alexandrov was such a scientist. Vladimir Alexandrov disappeared.

THE HOUSE OF RE-ANIMATION

A Soviet journalist was convinced the CIA kidnapped Vladimir Alexandrov in order to make him admit Nuclear Winter was not as catastrophic as he had once claimed.

The journalist visited a CIA house in New Hampshire Avenue, Washington DC. The house had been nick-named 'The House of Re-animation' because here CIA 'victims' were thought to have had their old memories washed away and be 're-animated' with new ones.

He wrote a report describing his visit to this house. In his report he mentions talking to a woman called Mrs Abbot who, after being questioned by him, denied all knowledge of ever having met a Vladimir Alexandrov.

The journalist's report also claimed that the CIA spend time hunting for Soviet and Eastern scientists who have valuable research information. They kidnap them, fill them full of drugs (or terror) then send them to this house. They are then forced to sign a form claiming they want to defect to the USA. CIA agents follow them so they cannot contact friends or colleagues and attempt to escape back to their homelands.

Searching For The Truth

One of the problems with Vladimir Alexandrov's story is that many of the 'facts' are in dispute. Here are some of the contradictions that have puzzled investigators over the years:

Version One

1. The Russians claim that Alexandrov was a drunk.

2. The Soviet government claim to have done everything they could to find their missing scientist.

3. The Soviet Embassy in Madrid have no record of being contacted by the Cordoba officials about Alexandrov's behaviour.

4. Alexandrov was not restrained in any way by his comrades.

Version Two

1. His American colleagues say he was not.

2. There were no formal requests from the Soviets to the Spanish to treat the case as a priority.

3. The Cordoba authorities called the Soviet Embassy in Madrid to express their concern over the conduct of an eminent Russian scientist.

4. Alexandrov ran away from the Embassy and had to be dragged back by an official.

5. Alexandrov was treated with care at all times during his trip to Spain.	5. The scientist was bundled into a van by members of the KGB.
6. His wallet was found in his room.	6. His wallet (and passport and airplane tickets) were found in a trash can near the hotel.
7. He was driven to Cordoba in a taxi.	7. He was driven to Cordoba by José Moreno, a driver for Cordoba City Council in a council car.

EPILOGUE

What happened to Vladimir Alexandrov?
For many months there was silence. The Spanish newspapers did not report the disappearance of the Soviet scientist. His friends and colleagues in America did not report it either. They stated that they kept quiet because if he was trying to defect then he wouldn't want to have any media attention, and, any publicity would only help the KGB to catch him... by staying silent they would give Alexandrov time to get safely to America.

His Soviet friends kept quiet too. Even his wife remained silent for a year before writing to Senator Edward Kennedy.

Most importantly, the Secret Services remained quiet. Neither the Soviets nor the US seemed to know where Alexandrov was. Each appeared to suspect that the other side had him. Neither wanted to make a public search until they were sure.

Finally, after three months, his Soviet and US colleagues realised that Vladimir Alexandrov was truly 'missing' and they began to make it public. On 17 July 1985 (105 days after he was last seen) a story appeared in the *New York Times*.

The Soviet Embassy could not conceal their ignorance – or intrigue – any longer.

Shortly after they asked the Spanish authorities to look for him. It wasn't until December 1985 that the Soviet press were finally allowed to publish the story. Naturally the Soviet press blamed the CIA for helping Alexandrov to defect.

If he had defected the CIA would no doubt have paraded him proudly in public. But the CIA didn't say that... because it would appear that they didn't have him.

So, if the CIA didn't help Vladimir Alexandrov reach the USA, and if the KGB didn't drag him back to Moscow, where did he go?

There was only one other person who could have arranged for the Soviet Nuclear Winter Man to disappear. That person was called Vladimir Alexandrov.

Vladimir Alexandrov had been living the life of a successful, internationally acclaimed scientist. He had been treated as a celebrity with appearances before the US congress and an invitation to visit the Pope. But that world was about to collapse around him.

His wife was ill. Life in Moscow was miserable with a sick wife and daughter. It seemed probable that life in Moscow was about to become much worse for all of them. When he returned he would no longer be regarded as a highly successful nuclear scientist. Did he think that it would be better for everyone if he didn't go home?

87

What had gone wrong?

What had gone wrong was Vladimir Alexandrov had been too passionate in his claims about the horrors of Nuclear Winter. He hated the thought of nuclear war. The more he studied the effects of blast and heat and radiation the more he felt he had to argue for peace. His own specialist skills were to do with climate. He supported the US scientists when they originally proposed the Nuclear Winter theory in 1983. But his calculations went further than theirs. He believed that Nuclear Winter would be *worse* than anyone had *ever* suspected.

But as scientific knowledge grew the evidence against his theory seemed insurmountable. Gradually, the US scientists, while respecting him, stopped believing in him. The Soviet scientists stopped believing in him. . . *and* probably stopped respecting him. He would undoubtedly be refused a place of honour in the Academy of Sciences.

If he went back to Moscow he faced a 'career winter'. He was finished. The only way out was to get out. To leave this life behind and start again. The CIA had stopped him using their super-computers; they obviously didn't trust him. If he went to the USA he'd always be treated with suspicion.

No, he had to go somewhere else – anywhere but the US or Moscow.

He decided to arrange his own disappearance. To give his talk in Cordoba

88

then simply walk away, make a new life for himself in a quiet part of Europe. The thought of doing this made him nervous. He drank heavily to calm his nerves.

Vladimir Alexandrov's conference speech in Cordoba was unfocused and rambling... his mind was on other things. He headed back to Madrid and hoped to board a plane to freedom. But the car was taking him back to the Soviet Embassy! He thought of the worst thing that could happen to him... they'd take him into the Embassy and keep him till the Moscow plane was due. They'd put him on that plane and he was finished!

He tore at the door handle and tried to get out of the car. He ran away from the Embassy but someone caught him and explained to him that they were just taking him to his hotel.

Once there he dumped all of his identity papers and passport in a trash can – inside or outside the hotel, it doesn't matter – and he walked off into the night.

His pockets were filled with US dollars. He could take a taxi to the airport and a flight to anywhere in Europe. With the money he'd saved he could pay, if he had to, for his new hosts to keep his secret while he set up a new life in a new country.

All he left behind was a mystery.

A mystery with the facts contained in KGB and CIA files. Files marked 'Unsolved'.

Files marked **CLASSIFIED**.

CLASSIFIED

Reader, your brief is to be on the alert for the following spine-tingling books.

CLASSIFIED SERIES:

☐ The Internet Incident	Ian Probert	£2.99
☐ Encounter on the Moon	Robin Moore	£2.99
☐ Discovery at Roswell	Terry Deary	£2.99
☐ The Philadelphia Experiment	Terry Deary	£2.99
☐ The Nuclear Winter Man	Terry Deary	£2.99
☐ Break Out!	Terry Deary	£2.99

Stay tuned for further titles. Over and out.